KU-518-995

This book belongs to:

_____

Contents

Cover illustration by Tania Hurt-Newton
Illustrations on pages 32-33 by Peter Stevenson

Published by Ladybird Books Ltd
80 Strand London WC2R ORL
A Penguin Company

4 6 8 10 9 7 5 3

© LADYBIRD BOOKS LTD MCMXCVII, MMI

LADYBIRD and the device of a Ladybird are trademarks of Ladybird Books Ltd

Printed in Italy

Tiger clouds

written by Catriona Macgregor

illustrated by Sumiko Davies

I can see a
big cloud.

It looks just
like a tiger.

Now it looks just
like a bear.

Now it looks just
like a monster.

Now it looks just
like a bird.

8

Now it looks just
like a face.

Now it looks
like rain.

Mess?
What mess?

written by Shirley Jackson
illustrated by David Pattison

I like helping…

Don't make a mess.

I like mixing…

Don't make a mess.

I like pouring…

Don't make a mess.

I like tasting…

Don't make a mess.

I like baking…

Don't make a mess.

I like eating…

Don't make a mess.

Mess? What mess?

Just look
at that!

written by Shirley Jackson

illustrated by John Dillow

Just look at that!

Just look at that!

Just look at that!

Just look at that!

What a good party.

My favourite colour

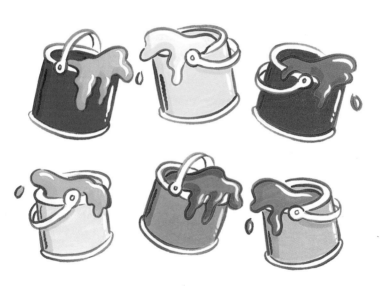

written by Catriona Macgregor

illustrated by Tania Hurt-Newton

He likes blue and

she likes yellow.

He likes red and

she likes green.

He likes pink and

she likes brown.

But **I** like them **all!**

New words introduced in this book

baking

eating

helping

mixing

pouring

tasting

brown

green

blue

all, but, he, looks

Just look at that!

All the words used in this story have already been met
in earlier books in the series. Join in together with the
speech bubbles. Encourage your child to read this story
with expression. The exclamation mark after 'Just look
at that!' shows your child that a loud and lively voice
should be used.

We like colours

This short story introduces your child to reading
several colours and the pronouns 'he' and 'she'.
What is your child's favourite colour?

New words

These are the words that help to tell the stories and
rhymes in this book. Try looking through the book
together to find some of the words again. (Vocabulary
used in the titles of the stories
and rhymes is not listed.)

Read with Ladybird

Read with Ladybird has been written to help you to help your child:

- to take the first steps in reading
- to improve early reading progress
- to gain confidence

Main Features

- **Several stories and rhymes in each book**

This means that there is not too much for you and your child to read in one go.

- **Rhyme and rhythm**

Read with Ladybird uses rhymes or stories with a rhythm to help your child to predict and memorise new words.

- **Gradual introduction and repetition of key words**

Read with Ladybird introduces and repeats the 100 most frequently used words in the English language.

- **Compatible with school reading schemes**

The key words that your child will learn are compatible with the word lists that are used in schools. This means that you can be confident that practising at home will support work done at school.

- **Information pullout**

Use this pullout to understand more about how you can use each story to help your child to learn to read.

But the most important feature of **Read with Ladybird** is for you and your child to have fun sharing the stories and rhymes with each other.